TONE WIKBORG

Gustav Vigeland

His Art and Sculpture Park

Translated by Ruth Waaler

ASCHEHOUG

CAPTIONS

Dates of the sculptures are referring to the original model in clay or plaster. The measurements are given in cm either in H = height, or in the following order: height × width. Owner of the works and photos is Vigeland Museum unless otherwise stated.

1. Self-portrait. 1922. Bronze. 45 × 18 × 20,5. Photo Jo Grim Gullvåg
2. Hell. 1897. Bronze. 171 × 380. National Gallery, Oslo. Photo Væring
3. Job. 1889. Pen. 32 × 15
4. Boy supporting drunken man. 1895. Pencil. 12,5 × 7,5
5. Young girl. 1892. Plaster. H. 162
6. Hagar and Ishmael. 1889. Plaster. H. 77
7. Accursed. 1891. Plaster. H. 174. Photo Koremasa Nakao
8. "Fear". 1892. Bronze. H. 29,5. National Gallery, Oslo. Photo Væring
9. The Resurrection. Detail of relief. 1900. Plaster. 167 × 352. Photo Knut Bry
10. Figure studies for the Resurrection. 1898. Pen.
11. Man and woman. 1893. Clay. H. 27,4. National Gallery, Oslo. Photo Væring
12. Man with a woman on his lap. 1897. Bronze. H. 47. Photo Teigen
13. The Newborn. 1903. Bronze. H. 47. Photo Teigen
14. Orpheus and Euridice. 1899. Bronze. H. 67. Photo Teigen
15. Man and woman. 1901. Pen. 20,8 × 14,5
16. Man and woman. 1901. Pen. 20,8 × 15,2
17. Man and woman. 1901. Pen. 20,9 × 14,9
18. Angel choking a basilisk. 1898. Plaster. Model for one in a series of gargoyles in soapstone, Nidaros cathedral, Trondheim
19. Monument to N.H.Abel. 1905. Bronze. Erected 1908 in the Palace Park, Oslo. H. 410 (with pedestal 1210). Photo Koremasa Nakao
20. Ludwig van Beethoven. 1906. Bronze. H. 153. Photo Koremasa Nakao
21. Henrik Ibsen. 1903. Plaster. H. 48,5
22. Man and woman. 1906. Marble. H. 191. Photo Kim Hart
23. Man with a woman on his lap. 1905. Bronze. National Gallery, Oslo. H. 132. Photo J.G. Gullvåg
24. Man with a woman on his lap. Pen. Ca. 1913. 22 × 14. Inscribed, "Sten" ("Stone")
25. Young girl. Detail of the group "Frightened". Ca. 1914. H. 67. Photo Paul Brand
26. Mother and child. 1909. Marble. H. 137. Photo Mittet
27. Recumbant lion. Ca. 1917. Woodcut. 10,5 × 19,5
28. Man and woman. Evening by the sea. 1928. Woodcut. 15,8 × 29
29. Waves breaking against cliffs. Ca. 1928. Woodcut. 19 × 39
30. Three girls. Ca. 1915. Woodcut. 30 × 19,5
31. Girl in old windblown pine. Ca. 1936. Woodcut. 32 × 16
32. Woman in front of a turf hut. Ca. 1933. Woodcut. 16 × 31,8
33. Woman riding and two men. 1931. Woodcut. 17,3 × 33,5
34. The Fountain, Vigeland Park. Photo Mittet
35. Vigeland Park. Photo Husmo
36. The Fountain and part of the surrounding mosaic labyrinth
37. Swarm of genii. Fountain tree group. 1912. Bronze. H. 200
38. Swarm of genii. Ca. 1905. Pen. 21,8 × 14. Inscribed, "They shall hang like a clump of swarming bees"
39. Children playing in the pool surrounding the Fountain
40. Small boy. Detail of a Fountain tree group. 1911. Bronze
41. Old woman and small child. Fountain tree group. 1908. Bronze. H. 200. Photo Harald Medbøe
42. Four children playing with a wolf. Fountain relief. 1935–36. Bronze. 55 × 60
43. Man kicking a wolf. Fountain relief. 1930–35. Bronze. 55 × 60. Photo Kim Hart
44. Woman and unicorn. Fountain relief. 1906. Bronze. 55 × 60. Photo Harald Medbøe
45. Woman between man and child. Fountain relief. 1923. Bronze. 55 × 60
46. Decaying skeletons. Fountain relief. 1915. Bronze. 55 × 60
47. Genius standing on the cranium of prehistoric animal. Fountain relief. 1916. Bronze. 55 × 60
48. Woman with tendrils and man with rope. Wrought iron gate. 1933–37. H. 245. Photo H. Medbøe
49. Circular stairs, granite groups and the Monolith. Photo Koremasa Nakao
50. Man and woman with child between them. "The Family". 1917. Granite. H. 160. Photo Johan Berge
51. Woman bending over many children. 1918. Granite. H. 159
52. Woman and children. Pencil. Ca. 1915. 14,2 × 21,8
53. Two boys plaguing an old mentally retarded man. 1923. Plaster, model for granite group. H. 182
54. Man hurling a woman. 1918. Granite. H. 100. Photo H. Medbøe
55. Old woman sits resting against old man. 1919. Granite. H. 177. Photo Kojan/Krogvold, Statens Filmsentral
56. Old woman and young man. "Mother and son". 1918. Granite. H. 159
57. The Monolith. Detail upper part
58. Transport of the Monolith block on two barges up the Oslo fjord, September 1926
59. The Monolith-block being raised. August 1928
60. The Bridge in Vigeland Park. In the foreground, Monk struggling with a lizard. Ca. 1930. Granite. Photo Kojan/Krogvold, Statens Filmsentral
61. Angry small boy. 1930. Bronze. H. 100. Photo Mark Sadan
62. Angry small boy. 1901. Pen. 20,4 × 16
63. Small child. 1940. Bronze. H. 42,5. Photo Ragnar Utne
64. Unborn child. 1923. Bronze. H. 41,5. Photo Mark Sadan
65. Man playing with small boy. 1928–30. Bronze. H. 210. Photo J. Berge
66. Running woman carrying a child in outstretched arms. 1928–30. Bronze. H. 200. Photo H. Medbøe
67. Running man with boy on his back. Ca. 1930. Bronze. H. 196. Photo Knut Bry
68. Running woman carrying girl in her arms. Detail. 1927. Bronze. Photo Knut Bry
69. Man and woman inside a ring. 1930. Bronze. H. 242
70. Man inside a ring. 1930. Bronze. H. 242
71. Angel struggling with dragon. 1898. Pen. 16,5 × 21. Inscribed, "Trondhjem Domkirke" (Trondheim Cathedral)
72. Lizard embracing woman. 1918. Granite. H. 230
73. Two dragon-fish fighting, biting each other's tail. 1928 Detail from wrought iron gate at the entrance to Vigeland Park
74. Entrance gates to Vigeland Park. 1926–34. Granite and wrought iron. Greatest H. 9,8 meter. Photo Jo Grim Gullvåg
75. Lizards and human figures. Six reliefs on bronze door to one of the gate houses at the main entrance. 1942. 200 × 95
76. The Sundial and the Wheel of Life. The signs of the zodiac are carved in relief on the granite plinth of the Sundial. Ca. 1930. The Wheel of Life was modelled in 1934. Bronze. Diameter 3 meters. Photo Jo Grim Gullvåg
77. Young girl encircled by lizard. 1938. Plaster model for bronze group in Vigeland Park. H. 156
78. The Clan. 1936. Bronze. H. 321. Height of pedestal 4 meters. Photo Asbjørn Tynning.
79. Vigeland Museum
80. Gustav Vigeland in his new studio at Frogner. 1924

© H. Aschehoug & Co. (W. Nygaard) 1990
Translated from Norwegian by Ruth Waaler

Second printing 1992

Grunnskrift 11/12 pkt. Times
Papir: 150 g Silverblade
Printed in Norway
Emil Moestue as, Oslo 1992

ISBN 83-03-17001-3

CONTENTS

INTRODUCTION

1

1 Self-portrait. 1922

Gustav Vigeland (1869–1943) has been characterized as the least known and most controversial sculptor in modern times. Although an unusually productive artist, few of his works are to be found outside Norway. Today, however, the sculpture park that he created in Oslo attracts large and ever-increasing numbers of people from all over the world. Here, nearly 200 of his bronze, granite and wrought-iron sculptures are placed in a 75 acre parkland designed by the artist himself. This exceptional sculpture park has always been a source of contention. Yet it is undeniable that Vigeland has struck a particular chord to which the general public responds. As available literature about the artist in any language other than Norwegian is scarce, the object of this publication is to give a general introduction to Vigeland's art and a more detailed coverage of the sculpture park.

Vigeland's work belongs within the humanistic tradition in art. From beginning to end he has been preoccupied with man at all stages of life and in his most fundamental relationships as they exist everywhere and at all times. His art is both subjective and universal; subjective because through his highly emotional nature he conveys personal experiences and insights; universal because people of all ages recognize themselves in his sculptures.

Vigeland's figures have a timeless quality in that almost all are nude and therefore detached from historical or social context. But, as all art, Vigeland's is the result of the times in which it was created. Vigeland's point of departure was the 1890s, a period of reaction to realism in art; a period in which attention was focused on the expression of the human psyche. Another tendency was the desire to find pictorial expression for thoughts and ideas of a more universal character and Symbolism as an art movement made a considerable impact on Vigeland. It is of interest to note that Vigeland was thirteen years younger than Sigmund Freud and six years older than Carl G. Jung. It may well be said that in his sculptures Vigeland, too, analyses emotions and instincts as well as fundamental relationships such as those between man and woman, parent and child.

In rendering human emotions, the sculptor's means are more limited than those of the painter, who, in addition to creating figures can make use of colour and of the surrounding space. The sculptor must convey emotional content through the body's language, its postures, movements, gestures and facial expressions. The degree to which Vigeland varies these means in figural positions and compositions is remarkable.

Vigeland has said that he was born with the gift of sensibility but to find the sculptural form for its expression was a struggle. His work undergoes considerable stylistic changes throughout the years but in its development, generally follows the main trends in contemporary European figurative art. Non-figurative art, which rejected human forms and emotions, held little interest for Vigeland although some influence from Cubism is noticeable in his increasing use of geometric forms in decorative elements and figural compositions such as THE WHEEL OF LIFE. (Ill. 76) As late as 1932 his firm conviction was expressed in his question: "When will the characteristics common to all mankind ever go out of fashion?".

CHILDHOOD AND YOUTH

On the southern coast of Norway lies the little town of Mandal. There Vigeland was born on April 11, 1869 in a small, two-storey frame house which still exists. When Vigeland was a child, Mandal was still a lively trade and shipping centre. Salmon and timber were the main exports and the harbour was filled with sailing vessels from near and far. Times were good for shipyards and sailmakers.

Vigeland's parents came from a long line of peasants who for centuries had cultivated their small farms in Audnedalen to the west of Mandal. In the family there were several skilled wood-carvers and craftsmen who made furniture and ships' fittings as well as working their farms. Vigeland's father was the first in the family to earn his entire income from his craft. He ran his own furniture workshop employing varying numbers of journeymen and apprentices. With his towering figure and violent temperament, he was the dominating figure in the home. In Vigeland's early childhood his father was fanatically religious. The children were required to attend daily prayers and psalm singing. Vigeland recalls that if anyone dropped something or caused the slightest disturbance during prayers it was as if the heavens had fallen. The torments of hell, man's sinful nature and need of redemption

2

2 Hell. 1897

6

formed a substantial part of his childhood upbringing. "There was too much Satan and too little Jesus. Too much darkness and too little light, if one can be considered lighter than the other", Vigeland has written. His mother had a calmer nature and the four sons, of whom Gustav was the second, were all closely attached to her.

As a child Gustav Vigeland was frequently ill and bronchitis plagued him throughout his life. He did not excel at school except in drawing. Apart from this, school was a thorough bore and his intellectual capacities were never stimulated. But, he read voraciously on his own, making great use of the town library. He was captivated by the literature of Antiquity and memorized long passages from Homer's Iliad and Odyssey. When he found illustrations of sculptures he drew copies of them. It was, otherwise, the family Bible with illustrations by Michelangelo, Raphael and other great European artists which gave him his first introduction to art.

Radical changes were to take place in the economically and socially secure artisan milieu which formed Vigeland's background until he was twelve. His father's religious fervour abated, cooled by drink. A younger woman entered his life. As he developed tuberculosis, the workshop was neglected and fell into disrepair. Gustav, with his extremely sensitive nature, suffered from these family conflicts and often went to live with his maternal grandfather on the family farm near Mandal. Here he continued his woodcarving in which he had shown early talent. At the age of fifteen, his father took him to the capital where he was apprenticed to a professional woodcarver. In his free time Vigeland studied what little sculpture the city had to offer and his ambition to become a sculptor took a more decisive turn. But, as the workshop where he was employed shut down and his father became seriously ill he had to leave Oslo after only two years. The family moved to the farm where after a short time his father died. During the ensuing couple of years Vigeland contributed to the family income by means of his woodcarving but never gave up his longing to become a sculptor. He drew continuously and a lump of clay brought back from Oslo was constantly re-formed into new figures. His ideal at the time was the Danish Neo-Classicist Bertel Thorvaldsen whose sculptures Vigeland studied in books and in a booklet of drawing exercises. A textbook on anatomy was keenly studied and his imagination was fed by extensive reading. After two years he decided to leave and taking with him a suitcase filled with drawings he returned to Oslo. For a woodcarver work was hard to find and in the bitterly cold winter months he was often without food or a roof over his head. In desperation one February day in 1889, he gathered enough courage to visit the elderly sculptor Brynjulf Bergslien and produce his drawings. Bergslien showed immediate interest. He arranged for a small amount of financial support from some of the city's wealthy citizens and he himself gave Vigeland his first elementary instruction in modelling, plaster-casting and carving in marble.

3

EARLY WORKS

Already in the autumn of 1889 Vigeland's group, HAGAR AND ISHMAEL, showing the desolate mother and child, was accepted by the Annual National Exhibition and was well received by the critics. (Ill. 6) The harmonious calm and soft forms of the figures still bear the stamp of his admiration for Thorvaldsen and this mild and somewhat sentimental work reveals nothing of Vigeland's turbulent nature.

4

3 Job. 1889
4 Boy supporting drunken man. 1895

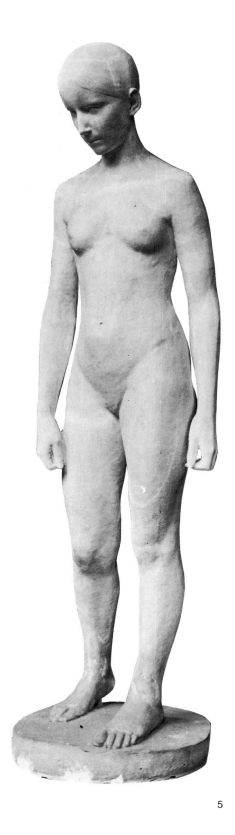

6

5 Young girl. 1892
6 Hagar and Ishmael. 1889

At the turn of the decade 1889/90, Vigeland began in the studio of Mathias Skeibrok. Skeibrok was also his teacher at the Royal School of Drawing where, for a time, he had followed classes in drawing and modelling. At that time there was still no Academy of Art in Norway and further studies had to be made abroad. Despite tough competition Vigeland received several travel grants. Unlike most of the others he never attended an academy nor studied with an established artist but preferred to work and study on his own in museums and at exhibitions. He was a keen observer and his letters home show a marked ability to formulate his impressions and opinions.

Vigeland spent 1891 in Copenhagen where he worked on a large sculpture composed of five life-size figures; its title CAIN was soon changed to ACCURSED which lent the composition a more universal dimension. (Ill. 7) The figures are shown in strong forward movement into space. The main figure is the suffering old man, his open and distorted mouth and face half covered by one hand. A boy, looking back in fear, runs beside him and on his other side a woman walks along with a sleeping infant in her arm while between them a faithful dog follows them

9

← 7   8

in their flight. Apart from the drapery arround the loins of the old man the figures are nude. There is a certain lack of stylistic uniformity in this work; the idealized character of the woman clashes with the pronounced realism of the old man whose figure reflects more thorough studies from live models. It was, nevertheless, quite an achievement on the part of this twenty-two year old sculptor, with only a few years of study behind him, to carry out a work of such dimensions and intense expressive strength. Although sculptures with pathetic content were not unusual at the time, this depiction of fear and suffering may also have been based on Vigeland's own sombre childhood experiences.

After his return to Norway in 1892, Vigeland created a more tranquil sculpture; the standing figure of a shy, young girl. (Ill. 5) Totally different again and yet from the same year is the statuette FEAR, a barely discernible female figure entangled in the clutching arm-like offshoots of a creature resembling a tree. (Ill. 8) Her mouth is open in a scream and the sculpture may be compared to Vigeland's six-year older countryman Edvard Munch's anxiety-laden paintings from 1892 and his expressive THE SHRIEK from 1893. Later, too, it is possible to find corresponding motifs in the works of these two artists.

In 1893, Vigeland spent five months in Paris where he rented a studio. During his stay he made several visits to the studio of Auguste Rodin. This encounter with the French sculptor's unconventional depictions of human emotions and passions became an important incentive for Vigeland. Rodin's GATES OF HELL inspired him to create his own version of this sombre theme in a 4 m wide and 1.8 m high relief entitled HELL, which was the central piece in Vigeland's first one-man exhibition in the autumn of 1894. We know this work only from photographs. In his travels in Italy in 1895/96, during which he studied sculpture from Antiquity and the Renaissance in particular, he realized that there were many weaknesses in the figural forms and remodelled the relief in 1896/97. (Ill. 2)

In the centre of the relief in a throne-like niche sits the brooding figure of a man whom Vigeland calls Satan. The space around him swarms with figures, young and old; they pour in from the right, moving towards the left side which is blocked by a gallows; only some faintly suggested figures float on above and beyond. At bottom centre some are falling into the abyss while above them a billow of figures swells toward Satan as if begging for an explanation of the existence of the power of evil and death. "The relief presents every phase of human suffering – the artist could just as well have called it Life as Hell", wrote a contemporary critic.

Vigeland's plan of including HELL in a frieze with three other reliefs was never realized. The others were to be JUDGEMENT DAY of which there is a sketch model from 1894, THE RESURRECTION which was almost completely modelled in 1900 (Ill. 9) and SALVATION or PARADISE which never got further than the drawing board. The idea, however, reappears in a clay sketch model of a cubic altar from 1923 where the reliefs are intimated on the four sides. The frequent religious motifs from his early years were otherwise to disappear.

11

9

10

9 The Resurrection. Detail of relief. 1900
10 Figure studies for the Resurrection. 1898
11 Man and woman. 1893

MAN AND WOMAN

11

The relationship between man and woman is a central theme in Vigeland's art. In a large number of drawings and sculptures he has depicted a wide range of emotions: attraction and affection, doubt and conflict, tenderness and combat. He created his earliest group of this kind, YOUNG MAN AND WOMAN (Ill. 11) in Paris in 1893. This suggests that Rodin's intimate, erotic sculptures had a liberating effect on Vigeland when he adopted this motif. The first man and woman groups are impressionistic studies in which content and expressiveness are stressed at the expense of sculptural form. Towards the end of the 1890s, however, his figures show improved proportions and more careful modelling. The beauty of Rodin's forms, however, never became a goal for Vigeland. His figures are elongated and emaciated; the skeleton is sensed beneath the thin layer of muscle. Examples from this period are MAN WITH A WOMAN ON HIS LAP, 1897 (Ill. 12) and ORPHEUS AND EURYDICE, 1899. (Ill. 14) These are not only typical of Vigeland's style at that time but of the spirit of melancholy and sorrow as well.

Vigeland also grasped a wider perspective in the man/woman relationship; they represent the regenerators of life itself. In his group THE NEWBORN, 1903, a man sits looking at a woman lying in front of him, a newborn infant on her stomach. (Ill. 13) When this group was created, Vigeland himself was the father of two children. The marriage, however, was short-lived and the children grew up under their mother's care. Yet, he was to create many superb sculptures of children and family groups. This suggests, perhaps, that through his art he compensated for the love and close contact he was unable to give in daily life.

12 Man with a woman on his lap. 1897
13 The Newborn. 1903

14 Orpheus and Euridice. 1899

12

13

14

14

15   16
17

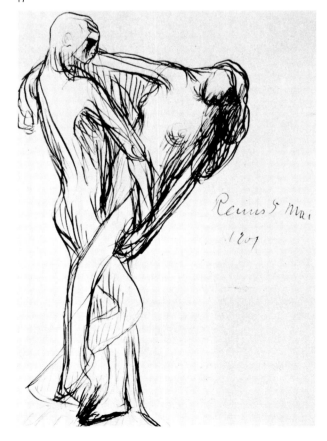

15 Man and woman. 1901
16 Man and woman. 1901
17 Man and woman. 1901

16

SCULPTURES IN "GOTHIC STYLE" (1898–1902)

18

18 Angel choking a basilisk. 1898
Plaster model for a gargoyle at Nidaros cathedral,
Trondheim

Although sculpture blossomed throughout the rest of Europe around the turn of the century, commissions were few and far between in Norway. The economic base was lacking and little interest was shown in this type of art. Vigeland's erotic groups and other nude figures were hardly suitable in the conventional bourgeois home and the possibility of selling was very limited. An attempt at applied art as more saleable resulted only in a candlestick in the form of a dragon and some drawings for vases and plates. "I can't stand this, I must get back to my human beings," complained Vigeland in 1896. In order to survive economically he applied in 1897 for work on the medieval cathedral in Trondheim which was under restoration and received orders for sculptures in "Gothic" style. In addition to the biblical figures above the screen-wall, he carried out a number of gargoyles in which he could give freer rein to his fertile imagination and sense for the grotesque. Inspired by medieval art he created his first representation of man struggling with a dragon, a theme to which he was to return later and imbue with a personal symbolic content. (Ill. 18, 60)

Two grants, for the study of Gothic sculpture in France and England made it possible for Vigeland to travel abroad in 1900 and to remain away for a whole year. Although he made conscientious studies of medieval art in a number of cities in both countries, his heart remained with his own art. Just as on other earlier visits abroad, this stay led to a turning point in his development. A considerable part of his time was spent in Paris and it is possible that renewed contact with Rodin's art was a catalyst. In more than 1,000 drawings made in the course of that year he let his imagination run free. They comprise a flood of ideas for figures, erotic groups, mythological motifs, fountains and monuments; an enormous fund of ideas from which he was to draw in the coming decades. (Ill. 15–17) Although the drawings were personal notes for sculptures, they have their own artistic value. The line became freer and more dynamic. In his letters home he reveals a new self-assurance and determination to carry out his own projects. After his return he lost interest in the cathedral sculptures which he now considered "pure humbug" and after 1902 he no longer accepted new commissions for the church.

MONUMENTS AND PORTRAITS

In the years immediately following the turn of the century Vigeland was to create several monuments and a series of penetrating portrait busts which consolidated his position as the country's leading sculptor. The memorial to the famous Norwegian mathematician N.H. Abel, who died at the early age of 27 in 1829, is Vigeland's first large outdoor sculpture. It was modelled from 1903 to 1905 and erected in the Palace Park in Oslo in 1908. (Ill. 19) Admittedly, the competition model from 1902 which is identical with the full-size sculpture caused considerable indecision and debate, even though the jury found the entry the most interesting as a work of art. It took several years for the committee to reach a decision but it is typical of Vigeland's new self-confidence that without waiting to obtain the commission he went ahead and modelled the 4 m high sculpture. Vigeland had chosen to ignore the competition requirements for a portrait statue. Instead he made a symbolic representation of the genius; the free flight of thought and fantasy through time and space. This abstract idea was created in the form of an idealized young man standing on the backs two male figures swooping downwards through the air.

Another example of an unconventional representation is the Beethoven statue from 1906. (Ill. 20) This dynamic, nude figure leans forward with outstretched arms in a conducting position, his torso bent as though weighed down by a heavy burden. The figure is characteristic of Vigeland's conception of the creative, struggling genius and exceeds the limit of any realistic programme. But, Vigeland has also created more traditional figural monuments with the subjects in contemporary dress while simultaneously managing to imbue them with personal expressions and a distinctive mood.

During the first decade of this century Vigeland also produced a remarkable number of other works, among them a succession of portrait busts of well-known Norwegian intellectuals including several versions of the dramatist Henrik Ibsen. (Ill. 21) Even though Ibsen, after the turn of the century was old, in poor health and only unwillingly sat to the sculptor a few times, Vigeland has accomplished a striking characterization of the agitated dramatist. An inner energy forces its way through the aging features which are rendered with impressionistic realism. The stylistic

19 Monument to N.H. Abel. 1905, erected 1908 in the Palace Park, Oslo

21

20 Ludwig van Beethoven. 1906
21 Henrik Ibsen. 1903

syntax of Vigeland's nearly 100 portraits, created during all periods of his artistic activity, varies greatly. The best of them, however, bear the mark of his psychological acuity and ability to convey an essential aspect of the model's character.

NEW TENDENCIES

An important change is to be found in Vigeland's work after the turn of the century. More and more he concentrated on creating larger sculptures intended for outdoor settings. In addition to the monuments, he created several life-size man and woman groups. In some groups he repeated motifs from earlier works in statuette size such as his MAN WITH A WOMAN ON HIS LAP in 1905. (Ill. 23) The figures remain slender but without the earlier accentuated leanness and Vigeland now shows a new interest in correct anatomical form. The emotional content of these groups, however, continues to show strains of the 1890s melancholy. Another group from this period is YOUNG MAN AND WOMAN from 1906. (Ill. 22) The two figures grow like branches from a common tree trunk. The man, his hands around her waist, holds the woman close to him but from waist up they both lean away from and look past one another. Despite close physical contact, they remain lonely individual figures. Several of these man and woman groups (Vigeland was averse to titles) are among the highlights of Vigeland's production both in treatment of form and analysis of complex emotions.

Unreserved affection, however, is to be found in the marble group MOTHER AND CHILD from 1909. (Ill. 26) in which a crouching woman holds a standing boy close to her. It is a psychological study of maternal love and the protective instinct as well as of the child's more divided feelings – the need for closeness and an awakening urge for freedom. The sculpture signifies another change in Vigeland's style. The female figure is more full-bodied than previously and a detailed naturalistic analysis is abandoned in favour of a simpler, more unified form. This tendency culminates a couple of years later at at time when Vigeland began to experiment with various kinds of stone. In a series of smaller than life-size crouching figures, carried out between 1913 and 1915, weight and massiveness as well as simplifi-

22 Man and woman. 1906

22

23 Man with a woman on his lap. 1905
24 Man with a woman on his lap.
Drawing for the group in stone. Ca. 1913

23   24

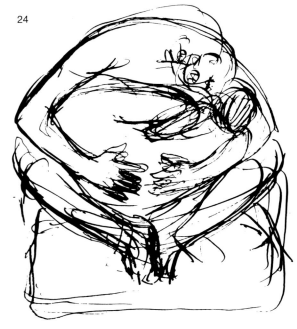

cation are characteristic features. (Ill. 25: detail of BOY AND GIRL, 1914. H. 67 cm). This transformation in Vigeland's stylistic form is clearly influenced by contemporary trends in European art. But, a number of the compositions have their roots in creations from the 1890s, thus revealing a continuity despite the apparent break with an earlier style.

From 1915 on Vigeland concentrated on the hard, pale grey, Norwegian granite which he found to be more suited to the Norwegian climate than other softer varieties of stone. He began a new series of groups, now over life-size, which later were to take their place in his sculpture park. Unlike many other sculptors of his day who maintained that direct carving of the stone was essential, Vigeland continued to model in clay and leave the rest of the work to professional craftsmen. His impatient creativeness was incompatible with the time-consuming process of carving.

During this period a new art form appears in Vigeland's work: the woodcut which he took up in 1915. He utilized his old skill

25 Young girl. Detail of the group "Frightened".
Ca. 1914
26 Mother and child. 1909

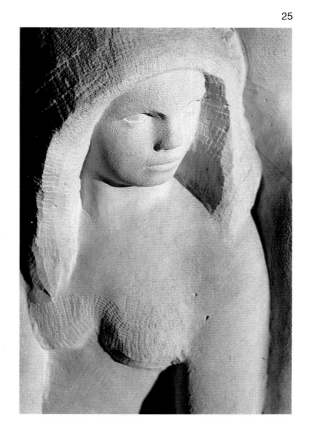

27

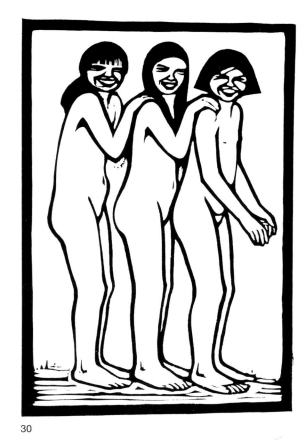

30

28

29

in woodcarving and his material consisted of ordinary household
breadboards of smooth-planed birch. His woodcuts, therefore,
are all more or less of a standard format. Vigeland never experi-
mented with colour nor with technical innovations as did Edvard
Munch. The cut, however, varies greatly from broad, black con-
tours to thin, subtle and elegant white lines. In the beginning
a flat surface style dominates and he repeats motifs from the
sculptures in a strong, decorative idiom (Ill. 30) or he recalls

27 Recumbant lion. Ca. 1917
28 Man and woman. Evening by the sea. 1928
29 Waves breaking against cliffs. Ca. 1928
30 Three girls. Ca. 1915

31

32

33

earlier animal drawings, with few but descriptive lines. (Ill. 27) Soon depth is added and landscapes become important. After his second marriage in 1922 to 19 year old Ingerid Vilberg, he spent several months each summer in his native district on Norway's south coast. From now on his favourite themes were scenes from the local landscape; the sea and foaming surf, the rocky sea-swept shoreline with its windblown trees. When Vigeland introduces animals and nude humans into this severe landscape, he depicts a primordial world far removed from civilization. (Ill. 31–33) In all, Vigeland produced some 420 woodcuts, the final ones in 1940. These were done in his spare time and made a welcome break from his work with the large sculptures and his increasingly comprehensive plans for a sculpture park.

31 Girl in old windblown pine. Ca. 1936
32 Woman in front of a turf hut. Ca. 1933
33 Woman riding and two men. 1931

VIGELAND PARK

A tradition of parks with sculptures stretches all the way from Antiquity to the present day. They were long the reserve and private pleasure of the aristocracy and wealthy citizens. In the 19th century public parks decorated with fountains and sculpture became more common. Modern sculpture parks usually function as outdoor museums representing the work of various artists. Vigeland Park differs in several ways from both earlier and more recent sculpture parks. It is totally the work of one man, created on his own initiative and without an original commission. Vigeland has not only modelled all the sculptures but has designed all the architectonic elements and the entire park plan. Vigeland Park, moreover, is a public park open around the clock.

As it stands today, Vigeland Park is not the product of an original co-ordinated vision. It is the result of a creative process in which additions have been made throughout nearly forty years. As the project developed, Vigeland's various plans were made public and submitted to the municipal authorities. This continuously led to intense debate but each time Vigeland's proposals were carried by a large majority in the Municipal Council.

The beginning was a fountain. In 1906, after working for several years on drawings and models, Vigeland exhibited a fountain model, including numerous sculptures, made in one-fifth the projected size. The public flocked to see it and the enthusiasm was overwhelming. A private committee was formed to collect money and in 1907 the Oslo Municipal Council passed a resolution to erect the fountain in the city centre in front of the Parliament. But, in 1916, at a time when the fountain sculptures were almost completed, Vigeland presented a plan for the addition of a series of granite groups to the fountain project which he now proposed placed in the Palace Park. In 1921 he suggested placing the fountain, the granite sculptures and the MONOLITH – his latest addition to the project – in front of his future studio and museum (See p. 60). Some of the politicians found this solution unsatisfactory and following an appeal from the Municipal Council, Vigeland worked out a new situation plan for an unbuilt area in connection with old Frogner Park. The plan was approved in 1924 and subsequently Vigeland's proposal for the main entrance, a considerable number of additional sculptures and substantial expansion of the park area.

Vigeland's plan for the park was, on the whole, complete in 1930 but many years were to pass before it was entirely fulfilled. Most of the sculptures are grouped in several large sections along an 850 m long main axis which conveys a strongly accentuated

34 The Fountain, Vigeland Park

35 View of Vigeland Park and its main axis. The actual sculpture park covers an area of 80 acres and contains 194 sculptures with more than 600 figures. It functions both as an art park and a public park. Here one skis in the winter, sunbathes on the lawns in summer and the park is very popular for walking and jogging the year around. Far to the right is the Vigeland Museum.

depth perspective; a transverse axis crossing the main axis at the fountain is less assertive. Long avenues of maples frame large, open lawn areas on each side of the main axis. Vigeland utilized the considerable height differences in the terrain by introducing terraces with sets of stairs leading up on either side. The strictly formal and geometric plan has several characteristics in common with French baroque gardens but in all probability Vigeland has been influenced also by the classisistic trend in the 1920s.

The Fountain

In order to give a better understanding of Vigeland's artistic development and shifting intentions, the various sculpture sections in the park will be described in an approximately chronological order. The earliest sculptures relate to the fountain (Ill. 34) and most of them were carried out between 1907 and 1913. The central group consists of six over-size men of different ages bearing a massive basin from which a veil of water spills down around them. (Ill. 36) The heavy basin may be interpreted as the burden of life borne with varying degrees of ability and willpower. Twenty groups of trees combined with human figures are placed in groups of five at the four corners of the pool. Broad and solid at the top while narrowing and opening up lower down, these groups correspond in form to the central group. A symbolic relationship exists as well; throughout time, water and the tree have always been associated to fertility and regeneration. In addition, the tree is a universal symbol of the life cycle which is the correlating theme of the groups at the corners of the basin and the 60 reliefs around its base. Each tree has its individual form and the asymmetrical, spreading branches bear the stamp of Art Nouveau. The tree as a motif was not new. It played an important role in the iconography of the 1890s and is a significant element in, for instance, Edvard Munch's "Frieze of Life" paintings. But, the combination of human figures and trees in large sculpture in the round was both a daring and original idea. The tree's branches and crown create a space around the figures allowing differentiated motion. Beneath the crown, light and shadow change with the weather and time of day, creating a romantic mood and lending an impressionistic character to the whole.

One of the tree-group themes is man surrounded by life-giving nature, another is the evolving stages of life from childhood to old age and a third is the life cycle and eternal regeneration. In this cycle of life, Vigeland utilizes both realistic and symbolic motifs. The series begins with a swarm of infants among the branches which may be interpreted as a symbol of life's inherent fertility. (Ill. 37) Vigeland usually calls such small imaginary children "geniuses" but in this case he has also called them "Angel

36

36 The Fountain and part of the surrounding mosaic labyrinth

32

Children" and in some drawings has given them small wings. In this introductory theme to the life cycle it may even seem that Vigeland visualizes a conception of pre-existence. He maintains, however, that his ideas are not the result of reflection but are subconscious: "They rise to the surface full-fledged like bubbles from the bottom of the sea."

In the following groups Vigeland has left the realm of fantasy and the children now belong to the real world; a boy sits listening in a tree, boys are climbing while girls stand quietly around the tree trunk. A return to fantasy concludes this section; a young girl, with a mixed expression of wonder and fear, glides

38

37 Swarm of genii. Fountain tree group. 1912
38 Swarm of genii. Ca. 1905
39 Children playing in the pool surrounding the Fountain

37

41

40

downward through the tree branches; a symbol of puberty. On the next corner of the basin the artist concentrates on youth. This section is flanked by a young woman and a young man standing dreamily each in their own tree. Between them, the groups portray various stages of love; the shy approach, a more hesitant situation in which the woman turns away from the man to be followed by a passionate embrace. (Ill. 39) Maturity is the theme of the third corner and includes several scenes of solitude as well as conflict. Among them are a man and woman falling downward, inextricably bound together by the branches of the tree. Here, as well, is one of Vigeland's finest portrayals of a child; an infant sits alone in a tree; a new generation has entered the cycle of life. (Ill. 40) Old age is the motif of the final corner. An old man and woman are shown standing, each with a child. The old woman in particular is portrayed with a penetrating realism which stresses the decay of old age in sharp contrast to the child's soft rounded form. (Ill. 41) In the penultimate tree in this last section a man clings to the tree of life. Finally, death appears, symbolized by a skeleton which itself has become a part of the tree.

36

40 Small boy. Detail of a Fountain tree group. 1911
41 Old woman and small child. Fountain tree group.
1908

42 Four children playing with a wolf. Fountain relief.
1935–36
43 Man kicking a wolf. Fountain relief. 1930–35
44 Woman and unicorn. Fountain relief. 1906
45 Woman between man and child. Fountain relief.
1923

A continuous sequence of 60 reliefs is set into the wall of the fountain. The constant delay in erecting the fountain gave Vigeland ample time to work on new ideas for these. In all, he created 112 relief plaques, the final one as late as 1936, before he made his final choice. Thus, they vary greatly in style both in the figural forms and in the utilization of the invariably plane surfaces of the background space. There is, nevertheless, a unifying idea which again is the cycle of life; all age groups are represented in a chronological development from childhood to old age and decrepitude. In this cycle appear a number of motifs depicting how humans relate to various animals: lambs, foals, eagles,

37

wolves, bears, reindeer, fish and the unicorn. Most of these reliefs are imaginary; even so they reveal Vigeland's views on the human relationship with nature, shown here in the form of animals. Children play trustingly with the wolf whereas an adult man fights with it and kicks it away. (Ill. 42, 43) Between women and animals, however, there exists a closer and more intimate relationship; she suckles the unicorn (Ill. 44), she is carried off on the back of a bear and sits sleeping in the reindeer's antlers. Apart from these, most relief motifs show typical, realistic situations from various stages of life. On these small plaques, 60×60 cm, Vigeland depicts eternally valid situations with

46 Decaying skeletons. Fountain relief. 1915

47

47 Genius standing on the cranium of prehistoric
animal. Fountain relief. 1916

striking simplicity as, for instance, a woman whose love and
attention are divided between a man and a child; while the lower
part of her torso faces the man kneeling before her she twists
around and looks to a small child. (Ill. 45)

The cycle of life, death and regeneration which succeed each
other in a perpetual process is even more clearly depicted in the
reliefs than in the tree groups. The gradual disintegration of dead
bodies extends through several reliefs ending in a few skeletal
remains (Ill. 46) but is immediately followed by a small genius
atop the skull of a prehistoric creature. (Ill. 47) The circle is
complete and life begins anew.

The 1800 m² area around the fountain complex is paved in stone mosaic in the pattern of a labyrinth. (Ill. 36) The final design, created in 1942, bears the stamp of Vigeland's late geometric style and is made up of 16 different circular zones, each framed by a square. The "Path" through the labyrinth follows the white stones from an entrance on the east side to the exit on the west. This maze is not purely a decorative element. It may be seen as a symbolic rendering of the path through life with its many turns and culs-de-sac and as such constitutes a meaningful appendage to the fountain sculptures.

The Monolith Plateau

Continuing along the main axis of the park and ascending the terraces, one reaches a large oval plateau. It is surrounded by a low balustrade broken by eight wrought-iron gates with figural compositions. These gates were conceived by Vigeland in the 1930s and forged by his expert smiths after his own designs. Each gate section is composed of either one or several figures. Children, adults or elderly people fill each panel, surrounded by a strictly stylized frame. Iron rods, 1.5 cm wide, are used with remarkable simplicity to outline the figures and carry out the organic details of bone structure, muscle, hair and even folds of flesh. Although these details often have a markedly ornamental character, they are still part of a realistic and evocative human portrayal. (Ill. 48)

48

48 Woman with tendrils and man with rope. Wrought iron gate. 1933–37
49 Circular stairs, granite groups and the Monolith

In the middle of the plateau a circle of granite stairs rises towards a platform from which 36 granite groups are placed in 12 radial rows on the steps. (Ill. 49) Once again it is mankind depicted within the framework of the cycle of life. On the topmost steps and axially directed toward the fountain, a group of many small children symbolizes the beginning of life while vis-à-vis a group of dead bodies depicts its end. Between these extremes Vigeland seeks to embrace central aspects of humanity. Compared to the fountain sculptures there are, nevertheless, considerable differences in these groups, which were carried out in the years between 1916 and 1936. Granite called for a totally different treatment of form than that required by bronze. In designing the compositions, the weight of the stone had to be considered as well as the fact that it was necessary for the figures to assert themselves in a large open space. The voluminous figures rest heavily on their plinths and in order to fit within the limits of the block they sit, kneel or bend over; only the children can stand upright. It is evident that Vigeland is aiming at a new monumentality. The powerful figures which seem to grow out of the mountain convey a sense of the primeval, possibly in accordance with the period's predilection for primitivistic vitality. In the earliest groups both figures and compositions reveal an endeavour to create a synthesis; the forms are extremely broad with little detail. (Ill. 50) Gradually, as Vigeland worked further with these groups, the forms became more differentiated, allowing naturalistic details to appear. (Ill. 56) With experience Vigeland learned

51

50

52

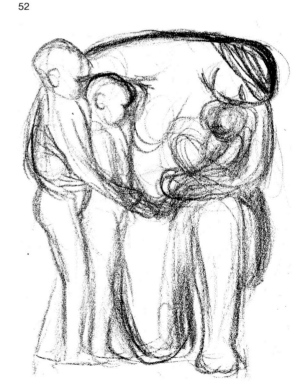

53

50 Man and woman with child between them. "The Family". 1917
51 Woman bending over many children. 1918
52 Woman and children. Drawing for a stone group. Ca. 1915

53 Two boys plaguing an old mentally retarded man. 1923

that the hard granite tolerated more than he had thought originally and also that he preferred a greater degree of analysis in depicting the human body. All the groups consist of two or more figures, their content concentrated on typical human relationships. The family motif plays a substantial role with its basic interpretation in the group of a man and woman who sit forehead to forehead holding an infant between them. (Ill. 50) The very personification of "mother earth", a woman bends down over a number of children who crawl in beneath her robust body. (Ill. 51) Vigeland has also depicted the world of childhood in an intimate and vivid way without lapsing into sentimentality. Children, however, are not merely small innocents; one of the groups shows two grinning boys persecuting an old, defenceless man. (Ill. 53) Further depicted is Eros' play with man and woman: attraction, embraces, the suspicion with which an older man regards a young, smiling woman, the devastating anger of a man hurling a woman away from him. (Ill. 54) But, Vigeland has also depicted lifelong ties in a group showing an old man tenderly supporting an old, reclining woman. (Ill. 55)

54 Man hurling a woman. 1918
55 Old woman sits resting against old man. 1919

56 Old woman and young man. "Mother and son". 1918
57 The Monolith. Detail, upper part

54

55

56

57

The eternal generation conflict is the theme of several groups: a father reprimands his son, a young man turns away in rejection from his old mother. (Ill. 56) In a number of groups, old age is depicted as a natural stage in human existence, sometimes with a crass realism which creates a pathetic picture of life's decline and transience.

The Monolith

In the centre of the circular area at the top of the surrounding stairs a 17 m high columnar sculpture surges upwards from the radiating granite groups. (Ill. 49) It consists of 121 human figures of all ages and Vigeland usually referred to it as "the human column". As, however, both the plinth and figural part are carved from a single stone, it soon became known merely as the MONO-LITH. The earliest model dates from 1919 and the last, which was the working model for the final sculpture, was made in 1923. The 13 m high figural section was modelled in three parts during 1924 and 1925 in Vigeland's new studio at Frogner. (See p. 60)

58

59

When the great rough stone pillar was raised into position in the park, a wooden construction was built, enclosing both the pillar and the full-scale plaster model. There, for most of the period from 1929 to 1943 three stonecarvers were engaged in transferring the modelled figures to the stone.

Seemingly dead figures lie at the bottom of the column. Figures then begin to ascend diagonally upwards to approximately the middle of the column where the spiral movement is broken by a number of figures who seems to be struggling not to fall back down again; a transversely placed man clings to a woman, an elderly man fights with two younger men. Following this, the figures continue to rise, but now straight upward. Approaching the top a man lifts a woman who gazes upwards as she stretches out her arms. Another young woman raises her arms with hands folded as if in prayer. The column reaches its climax in a swarm of small children.

The MONOLITH has been interpreted in different ways: a fertility symbol because of its phallic form, man's struggle for existence, a yearning for the transcendental, a vision of man's resurrection. Although Vigeland never directly expressed his intentions, certain statements indicate that his aim was to create a synthesis of his early compositions HELL and THE RESURRECTION. (Ill. 2, 9); he stated that rolls of photographs in which "the figures formed a column of ascending figures" gave him the idea. On another occasion he stated: "The column may be said to be related to Ruben's "Resurrection" and "Descent in Hell" and "Judgement Day" in the Alte Pinakothek, Munich." He wanted, however, to leave the interpretation to the spectator. Commenting on the sculptures on the steps as well as the MONOLITH, he said: "The stone groups depict life, the column belongs to the world of fantasy. Everyone, therefore, can understand the stone groups and each can interpret the column in his own way."

58 Transport of the Monolith block on two barges up the Oslo fjord, September 1926
59 The Monolith-block being raised. August 1928

46

The Bridge and the Children's Circle

60 The Bridge in Vigeland Park. In the foreground, Monk struggling with a lizard. Ca. 1930

Vigeland was barely finished modelling the figures for the **MONOLITH** when he embarked upon his plan for the main entrance to the park and the bridge over the ponds. The 58 sculptures to be placed on the parapets of the bridge were modelled between 1926 and 1933. (Ill. 60) Each consists of one or more figures and their arrangement on the parapets follows a strictly formulated plan. Calm, static figures are placed on either side of the bridge lanterns and in the intervening spaces are figures in dynamic action. All face either inwards toward the course of the bridge or their movements run parallel to it. In this, the park's third sculpture unit, there is no connecting life-cycle theme as in the fountain and granite sculptures. The only sign of

63

61   62

48

64

old age is in two older but otherwise extremely vigorous men. But, life's genesis is depicted in the centre of the children's circle below the bridge; in this case realistically by a fully-developed unborn child. (Ill. 64) Around the edge of the circle are eight small children in postures typical of life's first year. On the bridge are older children who have now begun to relate actively to their surroundings. An illustrative example is «SINNATAGGEN» (ANGRY LITTLE BOY) which is probably Norway's most popular sculpture. (Ill. 61)

A distinctive feature of the bridge sculptures is the many single figures; children, women and men. Another feature is the powerful, physical motion in many of the figures and an exuberant, extrovert joy in life which is something new in Vigeland's art. Otherwise, a diverse range of emotions and moods is also to be found in these figures on the bridge. Some few fundamental human relationships dominate in the groups. One is the mother/child and father/child relation and adults playing with children or protecting them is repeated in many variations. (Ill. 65–68) Another is the man and woman relationship which alternates between affection and conflict. Midway, on each side

61 Angry small boy. 1930
62 Angry small boy. 1901
63 Small child. 1940
64 Unborn child. 1923

65 Man playing with small boy. 1928–30
66 Running woman carrying a child in outstretched arms. 1928–30

67 Running man with boy on his back. Ca. 1930
68 Running woman carrying girl in her arms. 1927

67

68

69 Man and woman inside a ring. 1930
70 Man inside a ring. 1930

69

70

of the bridge, are two circular sculptures with symbolic themes. In one, a man and woman grasping each other's legs, rotate within a ring. It may be seen as representing the eternal attraction between the sexes as well as depicting man and woman or the masculine and feminine as an indivisible unit, a sort of personification of the Far East's concept of yin and yang. In the other circle a man struggles to break out. (Ill. 69, 70)

In the bridge sculptures, Vigeland has emphasized a clear silhouette and unbroken linearity. The full-bodied figures are rendered with disciplined simplicity. In these figures Vigeland approaches a classisistic syntax but, at the same time, he has imbued them with emotions, energy and vitality which is his hallmark.

Each of the four corners of the bridge is marked by a tall granite pillar bearing a large granite group. Three of the groups form a series in which a man struggling with a huge lizard is eventually overcome while in the fourth corner a woman stands impassively in the embrace of the creature. (Ill. 60, 72) The motif of the robed man fighting with the dragon-lizard was already utilized by Vigeland as early as the end of the 1890s when he was working on sculptures for medieval Trondheim Cathedral. At that time the dragon or lizard was the unequivocal symbol of demonic forces. Later, in several drawings, he appears to associate this force with sexuality. C.G. Jung's interpretation of animal symbolism's general content as the expression of man's primitive instincts may also apply to Vigeland's groups of animals with humans.

72

71 Angel struggling with dragon. 1898. Inscribed, "Trondhjem Domkirke" (Trondheim Cathedral)
72 Lizard embracing woman. 1918

71

The Main Gate

73

During the same period in which Vigeland was working on the bridge sculptures, he also designed a monumental entrance to the park. In 1927 he exhibited drawings and some finished details of the seven wrought-iron gates. A substantial donation from Oslo Sparebank ensured the financing of the plan which was then approved by the Oslo Municipal Council. (Ill. 74)

Five of the gates are double, each section consisting of three circular panels in vertical order. The middle panels contain designs with lizards and other fantasy creatures in combat while the remaining panels, above and below, have purely decorative, ornamental motifs based on organic plant elements. The animal motifs seem to be inspired by woodcarvings on Norwegian stave church portals and medieval wrought-iron work, whereas the stylized, decorative panels stem from natural growths in the Art Deco style. This latter style is even more pronounced in the towering sets of lamps dating from the 1930s. From the gates, railings curve slightly outwards to the gatehouses on either side of the segmental forecourt. The bronze doors of the gatehouses are each decorated with six small circular reliefs depicting humans and lizards inextricably entangled. (Ill. 75) Even children are shown in the clutches of the lizards. It is possibly the primitive instincts and destructive forces which man carries within him throughout life which are symbolized here. These reliefs were carried out in 1942 during the German occupation of Norway, the year before Vigeland's death.

73 Two dragon-fish fighting, biting each other's tail. 1928. Detail from wrought iron gate.
74 Entrance gates to Vigeland Park
75 Lizards and human figures. Six reliefs on bronze door to one of the gate houses at the main entrance.

74   75

76

The Sundial and the Wheel of Life

Following the main axis of the park beyond the bridge, the fountain, the MONOLITH and approaching the far end to the west, one passes a sundial mounted on a twelve-sided granite base bearing circular reliefs of the twelve signs of the zodiac. A flight of steps leads to the final sculpture, THE WHEEL OF LIFE from 1934 which consists of four adults and three children. (Ill. 76) These figures are modelled on a colossal scale and entwined in a circular composition around a void. Here again is the theme of regeneration and the eternal life-cycle, the leitmotiv of the fountain sculptures and the granite groups, expressed in a single sculpture. THE WHEEL OF LIFE is mounted on a low, pyramidal plinth which lends it an almost floating and rotating effect.

77 Young girl encircled by lizard. 1938
78 The Clan. 1936

77

78

Sculptures off the Main Axis

In the 1930s Vigeland also created sculptures intended for locations other than along the main axis. Only three of these have found their place in the park: KNEELING GIRL ENCIRCLED BY LIZARD, YOUNG BOY AND GIRL LEANING OVER A WELL and a large rectangular group of 21 figures modelled on a colossal scale and called THE CLAN. This last group (1934–36) terminates the transverse axis which intersects the main axis at the fountain and marks the northernmost boundary of the park. At long last a gift from IBM made it possible to have the group cast in bronze and erected in 1988. At either end of the group stands a man as if on guard and between them figures of various ages are compactly disposed in smaller groups, all repeating the theme of protection. This motif, also found in the parent and child sculptures on the bridge, is here extended to encompass the enlarged family. The group may also be interpreted as the symbol of a nation which closes ranks when danger threatens. (Ill. 78)

An Appraisal

Vigeland Park has been the object of considerable negative criticism, not least by the intellectual élite. Objections have been levelled at the "megalomania" concept, the rigidity of the park layout and at the profusion of sculptures as well as their naturalistic form and human content. It cannot be denied that the wealth of sculptures and their proximity to each other, especially on the bridge and on the circle of stairs, makes it difficult to concentrate on any one particular sculpture. From the very beginning, however, the park has had its warm supporters and even though it continues to cause controversy, opinions have gradually come to the stage of showing greater nuances and the popularity of the park continues to increase. The remarkable number of sculptures finds an explanation in Vigeland's enormous creative urge and vast work capacity. With his deep interest in everything human, his aim was to depict a panorama and a vision of life as he saw it; a totality as well as its single moments. According to the artist: "The characteristics common to all human beings are the most important in art and poetry."

Vigeland Park is a rare synthesis of sculpture, architecture and nature. The artist's intention that there should be an organic integration between spectator and the sculptures has succeeded to an extraordinary extent.

GUSTAV VIGELAND AND THE MUNICIPALITY OF OSLO

The park is not alone the result of Vigeland's efforts. It is also a rare testimonial to a city which dared to support an unusual artistic project of such dimensions. Exceptional generosity was shown Vigeland not only by the municipal authorities but by other institutions and private donors. In addition, the municipality funded an almost palace-like studio for the artist when, in

79 Vigeland Museum
80 Gustav Vigeland in his new studio at Frogner. 1924

79

his work with the park sculptures, he needed new and larger working quarters. It was on Vigeland's own initiative that a contract was drawn up in 1921: Vigeland bequeathed his entire production and the original models of all future sculptures to the municipality; in return he was to receive a studio which was to become a future museum. He was, moreover, left entirely free to create at his own will. The income necessary to cover his private needs was acquired through commissions for portraits and monuments, the sale of woodcuts and of casts of, for the most part, small sculptures. With the exception of the fountain he refused all remuneration for the rest of the park sculptures.

In 1923 he was able to begin work in the new studio which, in addition, contained comfortable living quarters for him in the top storey of one of the wings. In accordance with Vigeland's own wish, the building has also become his mausoleum and the urn containing his ashes is placed in the tower above the main entrance. In the late autumn 1942 he began to model reliefs for the walls of his own burial chamber; the theme, for the last time, the evolving ages for life. This series was never completed. In January 1943 Vigeland suffered a heart attack and was taken to hospital where he remained until his death on March 12. In 1947 Vigeland Museum, close by Vigeland Park was officially opened to the public. Thus, once again, another of Vigeland's wishes was fulfilled; that as much as possible of his work should be preserved and as an undivided collection be made available for future generations.

80

BIOGRAPHICAL OUTLINE

1869 Born April 11 in the small southern coastal town of Mandal, the second of five brothers, the third of whom died when only 18 months old. His father was a master carpenter who ran his own furniture workshop where he employed apprentices but designed and carried out the woodcarving on the furniture himself.

1875–
1883 Attended school in Mandal but did not finish secondary school. Because of conflicts in the home, (his father, previously a stern religious pietist, had taken to drink and become involved with a young woman), he moved in December 1882 with his mother and youngest brother to his maternal grandfather who lived on a small farm at Vigeland, near Mandal. Attended the local school for a while and otherwise occupied himself with woodcarving and reading.

1884–
1885 Taken by his father to Oslo where he was apprenticed to a professional woodcarver for about two years. Attended evening classes in drawing at the Royal School of Design and visited the Sculpture Museum with its plaster casts of sculptures from Antiquity. His wish to become a sculptor himself seemed completely out of reach.

1886–
1887 Returned to Mandal spring 1886. His father died of tuberculosis in June and the family settled permanently on the farm at Vigeland. Helped with the farm work, did some woodcarving to sell and drew a great deal with a view to sculpture. Studied anatomy from books and read extensively, particularly literature from Antiquity.

1888 Returned to Oslo in October. Found work in a woodcarving workshop, but because of lack of orders was given notice Christmas Eve.

1889 A period of severe poverty and hunger ensued. In February he showed his drawings to the sculptor Brunjulf Bergslien who arranged some modest financial assistance through private sources and became his first teacher. In Bergslien's studio he modelled the group **Hagar and Ishmael** which was accepted by the autumn National Art Exhibition. Attended classes in modelling and drawing from life at the Royal School of Design. Carried out a couple of reliefs with Homeric motifs.

1890 Pupil of Mathias Skeibrok at the School of Design; also worked in Skeibrok's studio on the advice of Bergslien. Terracotta statuette **David** purchased by the Art Society and exhibited there. Carried out two orders for façade sculptures. Received a grant from Mandal Handicraft Association.

To Copenhagen in January where he was accepted into the studio of the sculptor V. Bissen. Here he modelled **Accursed,** his first group of life-size figures. Awarded a state grant in the spring, making it possible for him to remain in Copenhagen for the rest of the year.

1892 Returned to Oslo in February. Modelled the statue **Young Girl,** several statuette figures and his first portraits. **Accursed** was shown at the official Danish Spring Exhibition at Charlottenborg in Copenhagen and at Norway's official Autumn Exhibition in Oslo. Received state grant for the second time. To Copenhagen at the beginning of December; took lessons in French and continued on to Paris at the end of the month.

1893 Rented studio in Boulevard Gouvion St. Cyr 23 where he did a number of small sculptures. Studied on his own in museums, went to exhibitions and visited the studio of Auguste Rodin several times. Returned to Norway in June. Made the first designs for the relief **Hell**.

1894 The relief **Hell** (first version). Made several sculptures with biblical motifs, portraits and other works. Received a grant from Houen's Fund (first time). Compulsory military duty May–June. Held his first one-man exhibition October 20 to November 4 consisting of 51 sculptures.

1895 In Berlin for three months from beginning of February. Lived in the same hotel as Edvard Munch in Mittelstrasse 47; became part of an international group of artists and writers whose gathering place was the wine tavern, popularly called "Zum schwarzen Ferkel". Studied in the museums and made several sculptures, some of which he destroyed, among them portraits of Edvard Munch and Dagny Juel Przybyszewska. On to Florence where he stayed about a month. To Norway and further military service from June 10 to July 9. Grant from Houen's Fund (second time).

1896 Travelled direct to Florence in beginning of February. Studied art from the Renaissance and Antiquity, especially that of Egypt and classical Greece. In May, three week visit to Rome, Naples, Pompeii, Herculaneum and Orvieto. Left Florence August 21. Back to Oslo and started to model **Hell** once again.

1897 Military duty in June. **Hell II** completed in September. First monograph of Vigeland published in Berlin: "Auf den Wegen der Seele" by Stanislaw Przybyszewski. Modelled several **Man and Woman** groups in statuette size. Applied for commissions for restoration works on medieval Trondheim Cathedral.

1898 A series of sculptures in statuette size including **The Kiss, Amor and Psyche, Night, The Hermit.** Military duty in June.

November–December in Trondheim where he modelled 16 gargoyles for the cathedral main tower, among them **Man Fighting a Devil.**

1899 Received commissions for: an over life-size portrait of J. Schwarts, M.P. for an outdoor site in Drammen, a small **Standing Boy** for a fountain in Hamar, a private funerary monument, **The Angel** (completed in marble 1902). Modelled several figures for Trondheim cathedral exterior and four of the nine biblical figures for the choir screen-wall (**Moses, Isaiah, Elijah, Mary**). Daughter Else born June 21. Held his second one-man exhibition of 42 sculptures at Wang's Gallery in Oslo.

1900 Pro forma marriage to Laura Mathilde Andersen July 23. Executed the relief **The Resurrection** and the statue **The Worker.** Did a model for a fountain, a basin held aloft by six men. Grant from Houen's Fund (third time) for the purpose of studying Gothic art in France and England. Arrived in Paris November 5.

1901 January 21 was made Knight of the Order of St. Olav by King Oscar II. During January studied Gothic sculpture in Notre Dame, St. Chapelle and the Trocadero in Paris. Did a series of drawings for a large fountain with urns mounted on surrounding balustrade; also drawings for monuments, groups and figures. Spent February 1 to 9 in Chartres. Modelled portraits of two Norwegian authors and the **medal for the Nobel Peace Prize** in Paris during March and April. Son Gustav born in Norway March 27. To Rheims, Amiens and Laon in May and beginning of June. In London from June 14 to July 28 where he greatly admired Phidias' Parthenon sculptures in the British Museum. Visited the cathedrals in Salisbury, Wells, Somerset, Gloucester, Oxford, Ely, Lincoln, York, Selby, Howden and Beverly from the beginning of August until about October 20. Divorce decree signed August 29. Returned home end of October. Modelled the first of four portraits of **Henrik Ibsen.** To Trondheim December 29.

1902 In Trondheim until February 17. **The Crucifixion, David, John** and an **Angel** for the choir screen-wall were carried out; also **four reliefs of angels** for the arcades in the nave and four small reliefs for the baptismal font. Submitted entry to the **N.H. Abel monument** competition; in not meeting competition requirements it was not awarded a prize. Commissioned in July to do the **Nordraak monument** (Norwegian composer 1842–66). An old studio on Hammersborg, a height in Oslo, put at his disposal by the municipality.

1903 Thirteen portrait busts, among them **Edvard Grieg, Knut Hamsun, King Oscar II, Fridtjof Nansen, Henrik Ibsen** and **Alfred Nobel.** In April began a full-scale model for the **Abel monument** although not commissioned. Was made member of the board of directors of the National Gallery and the Sculpture Museum (until 1906).

1904 Continued work on the **Abel monument** and made several portrait busts.

1905 Completed modelling the **Abel** and **Nordraak monuments.** The committee for the erection of the Abel monument decided to acquire the sculpture. Did twenty small models of groups consisting of human figures and trees for a basin to surround the fountain. In July hiked in the mountain districts of Jotunheimen. In August made a trip to Paris with Inga Syvertsen, his close friend from 1900 on, housekeeper and assistant from 1902 to 1921.

1906 Carried out two life-size groups of **Man and Woman.** By request two models for a monument to **Camilla Collett** (Norwegian writer and feminist, 1813–95). Model for a **Henrik Ibsen funerary monument** (never realized) and a life-size sta-

tue of **Beethoven**, the latter cast in bronze at his own expense (Vigeland Museum). Divorce from Laura Mathilde became final on April 7. His brother Theodor died from tuberculosis on June 20. Hiked in Jotunheimen during summer. The fountain, 1/5 projected size, completed and exhibited in Oslo from October 14 to November 25. Made the first of the full-scale models of the twenty tree groups for the fountain; also several of the reliefs. The first "Vigeland Committee" began to raise funds for the erection of the fountain.

1907 His mother died April 10. Financial help to his brother Julius to enable him to take over the family farm at Vigeland. Monument of **Henrik Wergeland** (poet and writer, 1808–48) commissioned by the city of Kristiansand. Made small-scale models for several monuments, portraits and the life-size groups **Mother and Child, Kneeling Man Embraces Standing Woman;** also sculptures for the fountain which was commissioned by the municipality for the square in front of the Parliament. Short stay in Paris in August.

1908 In June **Henrik Wergeland** statue unveiled in Kristiansand and in Fargo, North Dakota. Began the commissioned statue monument of Camilla Collett. Short trip to Paris in the spring and to London and Copenhagen in October. The **Abel monument** unveiled in the Palace Park October 17. Small-scale model for an equestrian statue of **Theodore Roosevelt riding at a trot** (the expected commission by Norwegian Americans never materialized).

1909 **Camilla Collett** statue completed in February. From April to October modelled the six giants who support the basin of the **fountain.** Participated with four sculptures in a Norwegian exhibition in Copenhagen. Became interested in different kinds of stone and had samples sent from Copenhagen.

1910 Rheumatic attack and pleurisy in January. Suffered from rheumatism for about two years and was periodically unable to work. Did the final carving of two groups in marble and several portraits in soapstone. Participated with one group, **The Beggars** (1908), in an international exhibition in Brussels. Made designs for wrought-iron railing to surround two of his monuments.

1911 **The Beggars** included in an international exhibition in Rome. Made short trips to Stockholm and Copenhagen. His **Nordraak** and **Camilla Collett** monuments were unveiled in May.

1912 Finished several groups and reliefs for the fountain. Ordered blocks of limestone from Copenhagen.

1913–
1914 Modelled 33 "medium-size" groups of which 14 were carved in stone. Nothing came of a plan to send the groups to exhibitions abroad, probably due to the outbreak of World War I. Several of the motifs were later used in the series of large granite groups. Continued work on the fountain sculptures. Made short trip to Paris in May to see a Chinese exhibition.

1914 Did the first two full-scale models intended for a series of granite groups with over life-size figures. Modelled the last four of 20 tree groups for the fountain. Made the first drawings for a mosaic labyrinthine pavement in stone to surround the fountain. Visited Malmö, Sweden, in July to see a Baltic exhibition.

1915 Began making woodcuts. Finished three large models for the granite groups and carving was begun. His plan to place the fountain in the Palace Garden was made public in April.

1916 Announced his plan for an enlargement of the fountain project with a stair construction on which the granite groups were to be mounted. A model of the new project and some

finished groups were exhibited in his studio in April. A new Vigeland committee was established to finance the granite groups (modelled in full size 1915–36). Made a fountain sculpture with four lizards spouting water (granite, now in the courtyard of the Vigeland Museum). Did 23 reliefs for the fountain; of these, 14 were used.

1917 Exhibited 53 woodcuts at the Artists' Association in April. Modelled several portraits and seven full-size models for the granite groups.

1918 Finished ten full-size models for the granite groups.

1919 Made the first plastic sketch for the **Human Column** – the **Monolith**. Negotiations with municipal authorities about a new studio building.

1920 Made seven full-size models for the granite groups and **Woman Resting in the Antlers of a Reindeer.**

1921 Contract with the municipality signed in February. The municipality took over the ownership of all works of art in Vigeland's possession as well as original models of future sculptures and in return agreed to build a studio and future museum. Vigeland suggested that the **Monolith** be incorporated into the fountain project and presented a new plan for placing the whole in front of the future studio/museum building at Frogner. Broke off his 21 year relationship with Inga Syvertsen.

1922 February 22 married Ingerid Vilberg, born 1902. The City Council passed a resolution requesting Vigeland to suggest a site other than the one in front of the studio/museum for the fountain project. A new model was made, placing it west of the ponds in Frogner Park. A debate lasting nearly two years began. Appointed member of the Royal Swedish Academy of Fine Arts.

1923 Continued work on models for the granite groups and also twelve reliefs for the fountain, of which five were used. Appointed honorary professor of the Art Academy in Carrara. Began to work in the studio at Frogner in October.

1924 Moved into new living quarters in the studio building; from 1924 to 1926 made designs for wrought-iron lamps, candleholders and other items including textiles for his new home. Started work on the full-scale model for the **Monolith.** In November the City Council approved the site for the sculpture park according to Vigeland's 1922 plan.

1925 Made plans for extension of the sculpture park to include a main entrance and a series of sculptures for the bridge across the Frogner ponds.

1926 1926–33: 58 full-size models for figures and groups on the bridge.

1927 Drawings for the sculpture park's main entrance and some already forged details for the wrought-iron gates were exhibited for the Museum of Applied Art.

1928 The City Council approved the plans for the main entrance. A smithy was built outside the studio and three men engaged to carry out the wrought-iron gates for the sculpture park. Built a summer house on the coast near the familiy farm at Vigeland. The **Monolith** block was raised in situ.

1929 Presented with the Grand Cross of the Order of St. Olav on his 60th birthday. The carving of the **Monolith** was begun by three artisans in July (completed July 1942).

1930 A scale model of Frogner Park bridge with 62 sculptures, some already completed in full size, also plans for extension of the sculpture park area were exhibited to the public in Vigeland's studio from June 2 to 29.

1931 After yet another "Vigeland debate" the City Council approved the extensions of the sculpture park July 9. The first clearing and landscape work was begun.

1932 An exhibition of 131 woodcuts was held in the studio in October.

1933 Made first drawings of human figures for the wrought-iron gates to be placed on the Monolith plateau.

1934 Modelled **The Wheel of Life.** The upper parts of the wrought-iron gates for main entrance to the park were begun. The gates were finished in 1938 and mounted 1941–42.

1936 Did a colossal portrait statue of Prime Minister Christian Michelsen (1857–1925); erected in Bergen 1938. Modelled **The Clan**, a group of 21 over-life-size figures for the sculpture park; erected in bronze 1988.

1937 Carried out a statue of the Reformation clergyman, **Peder Claussen Friis**; raised at Valle Church near Vigeland as a gift from the artist.

1938 Modelled the statue of **Snorre Sturlasson** (historian and skald, 1178–1241) erected at Reykholt, Iceland in 1947 and in Bergen 1948. **Girl and Lizard**; mounted in Vigeland Park 1959.

1939 Executed a funerary monument **The Good Shepherd**, Vestre Aker Church, Oslo. Made honorary member of the Art Society. Began modelling **Man and Two Women in a Triangle** for the sculpture park (not erected). The bridge sculptures were mounted in the park 1939–40.

1940 Modelled eight figures of children for the Children's Circle beside the bridge and another **Triangular group** (not yet erected in the park). Separation from Ingerid Vigeland.

1941 Several sculptures executed for the park; these exist only in plaster in Vigeland Museum.

1942 Carried out twelve small reliefs of lizards and human figures for the doors of the gate-houses at the main entrance to the sculpture park. Modelled a **self-portrait statue** and during the autumn wall reliefs for his own mausoleum in the studio/museum building.

1943 Suffering from heart disease, he was admitted to hospital in January where he died March 12.

1947 Vigeland Museum was opened to the public. Installation of the fountain in Vigeland Park was completed.